DATE DUE			

EXPLORING SCIENCE

ATOMS & MOLECULES

BUILDING BLOCKS OF THE UNIVERSE

BY DARLENE R. STILLE

Content Adviser: Martin Feldman, Ph.D., Professor Emeritus, Howard University, Washington, D.C.

Science Adviser: Terrence E. Young Jr., M.Ed., M.L.S., Jefferson Parish (Louisiana) Public School System

Reading Adviser: Rosemary G. Palmer, Ph.D., Department of Literacy, College of Education, Boise State University

Compass Point Books • Minneapolis, Minnesota

Compass Point Books • 3109 West 50th Street, #115 • Minneapolis, MN 55410

Visit Compass Point Books on the Internet at *www.compasspointbooks.com*
or e-mail your request to *custserv@compasspointbooks.com*

Photographs ©: BSIP/Joupert/Photo Researchers Inc., cover; Chee-Onn Leong/Shutterstock, 4; Bol/Begsteiger/BSIP/Phototake, 5; Digital Art/Corbis, 6; Francois Paquet-Durand/Photo Researchers Inc, 7; Louis Psihoyos/Corbis, 8–9; Andrea Danti/Shutterstock, 10; Roger Russmeyer/Corbis, 13; Michael Wong/Corbis, 14; Michael Ledray/Shutterstock, 15; Mehau Kulyk/Photo Researchers Inc., 17, 33; Alfred Pasieka/Photo Researchers Inc., 19, 37; Laguna/Photo Researchers Inc., 20; Josiah J. Garber/Shutterstock, 21; Bettmann/Corbis, 24, 40; Calvin Larsen/Photo Researchers Inc., 25; John Durham/Photo Researchers Inc., 26; Boscariol/Photo Researchers Inc., 27; Ted Spiegel/Corbis, 30; Science Source/Photo Researchers Inc., 31; C. Powell, P. Fowler and D. Perkins/Photo Researchers Inc., 34, 41; NASA/Photo Researchers Inc., 35; U.S. Department of Energy/Photo Researchers Inc., 36; BSIP/Cortier/Photo Researchers Inc., 38; DOE/Science Source/Photo Researchers Inc., 43; CERN/Photo Researchers Inc., 44; Rich Treptow/Photo Researchers Inc., 46.

Editor: Anthony Wacholtz
Page Production: Bobbie Nuytten
Photo Researcher: Lori Bye
Cartographer: XNR Productions, Inc.
Illustrator: Farhana Hossain

Art Director: Jaime Martens
Creative Director: Keith Griffin
Editorial Director: Carol Jones
Managing Editor: Catherine Neitge

Library of Congress Cataloging-in-Publication Data
Stille, Darlene R.
Atoms & molecules : building blocks of the universe / by Darlene R. Stille.
   p. cm.—(Exploring science)
Includes index.
 ISBN-13: 978-0-7565-1960-5 (library binding)
 ISBN-10: 0-7565-1960-8 (library binding)
 ISBN-13: 978-0-7565-1966-7 (paperback)
 ISBN-10: 0-7565-1966-7 (paperback)
   1. Atoms—Juvenile literature. 2. Molecules—Juvenile literature. I. Title. II. Title:
   Atoms and molecules. III. Series.
   QC173.16.S74 2006
   539.7–dc22   2006027044

(About the Author)

Darlene R. Stille is a science writer and author of more than 70 books for young people. When she was in high school, she fell in love with science. While attending the University of Illinois, she discovered that she also loved writing. She was fortunate enough to find a career as an editor and writer that allowed her to combine both of her interests. Darlene Stille now lives and writes in Michigan.

TABLE OF CONTENTS

The Tiniest Wonders

THE WORLD IS a place filled with many natural wonders. Huge mountains rise from flat plains. Waves from the ocean lap against the sandy seashore. Eagles soar in the sky, and deer roam the grasslands and forests.

Some of the greatest wonders of nature, however, exist in a world that we cannot ordinarily see. They are found in the tiny world of atoms and molecules. Atoms cling together to form molecules, large

Even the smallest grain of sand is made up of millions and millions of atoms.

and small. This tiny, unseen world makes up all the visible matter in the universe, from mountains and oceans to the stars in the sky.

THE WORLD OF ATOMS

Everything in the universe is made of matter. An atom is a basic building block of matter. There are different kinds of atoms. A material made of just one kind of atom is called a chemical element. For example, iron is a chemical element made only of iron atoms. Oxygen and hydrogen are also chemical elements.

There are 91 natural chemical elements. Physicists have been able to make some artificial elements as well. Each natural and artificial element is made up of a different kind of atom.

Iron is an element made of only one kind of atom. Iron is usually a solid, but it can be melted at extremely high temperatures.

THE WORLD OF MOLECULES

Atoms of chemical elements join to make molecules. Some molecules, such as oxygen molecules, are made of two or more atoms of the same kind. Compounds consist of molecules that are made of different kinds of atoms.

Some molecules are small and simple. A molecule of water, for example, is made of two hydrogen atoms and one oxygen atom. Other molecules are large and made of many kinds of atoms. All living things are made of complex molecules, from cells and tissues to arms and legs. Molecules also control how living things work. We can run because of molecules. Molecules help carry messages from our brain to our legs. Our brain sends a message to start running. Special molecules carry the message

Deoxyribonucleic acid (DNA), the molecule that genes are made of, contains thousands of atoms.

from one nerve cell to another until it reaches the muscles in our legs.

For thousands of years, people have been asking the question: What is the world made of? We could say atoms and molecules, but scientists have found that things are not quite that simple in the world of basic building blocks. Inside atoms, physicists have found even smaller particles.

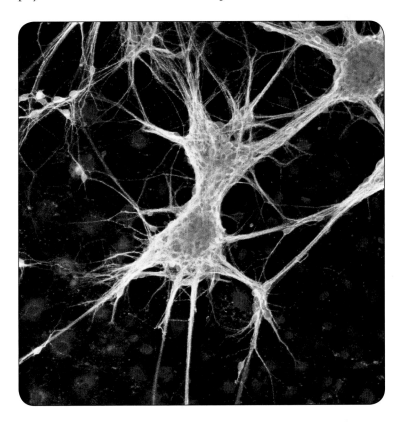

Molecules send messages from one nerve cell to another as the brain gives instructions to the rest of the body.

The Idea of Atoms and Molecules

It took centuries for scientists to learn about the atoms of each chemical element and how the atoms combine to form molecules of different substances. The idea of atoms began with ancient Greek philosophers. The Greek philosopher Democritus said that all matter was made up of invisible pieces that he called atoms. Differences in substances were due to differences in the size and shape of atoms.

The Greek philosopher Aristotle disagreed with the idea of atoms. He thought that everything was made of four elements—earth, air, fire, and water. Heat could change one element into another. Aristotle's ideas won out for thousands of years.

In the Middle Ages, a group of experimenters called alchemists helped pave the way for the science of chemistry. The goal of the alchemists was not to gain scientific knowledge, however. From ancient times, people knew about substances such as iron, copper, and gold, which we recognize as chemical elements. The alchemists believed that one substance could be changed into another. Their goal was to change lead and other metals into gold.

The alchemists invented many tools used by modern chemists, such as beakers, scales, and special pots for heating elements and compounds. They experimented with elements such as lead, mercury, and sulfur and learned about their properties.

The first real scientists, beginning in the 1600s, did not rely on guesswork. They formed hypotheses and tested them with experiments. They carefully weighed substances before and after chemical reactions. In the 1800s, they learned that elements combine in the same proportions to form molecules of new substances. For example, two atoms of hydrogen and one atom of oxygen combine to make one molecule of water.

Alchemists tried a variety of experiments to turn various elements into gold.

CHAPTER TWO

The Strange World of the Atom

AN ATOM IS made up of two basic parts. At the center is a dense core called the nucleus. Orbiting around the nucleus are one or more tiny particles called electrons, the smallest parts of an atom.

An atom is extremely small. It would take billions of atoms to fill the period at the end of this sentence. Nevertheless, if the nucleus of the simplest atom (hydrogen) had the diameter of a tennis ball, the diameter of the entire atom, including its one electron, would be 4 miles (6.4 km) across. Between the nucleus and the orbiting electron, there would be 2 miles (3.2 km) of empty space.

Electrons orbit around the tightly packed protons and neutrons in the nucleus.

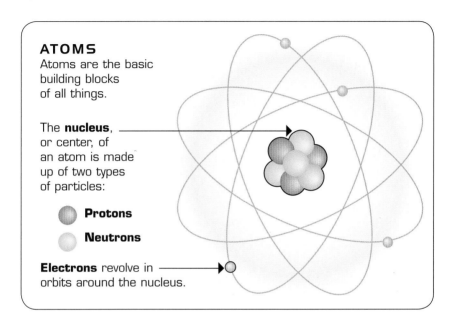

ATOMS
Atoms are the basic
building blocks
of all things.

The **nucleus**,
or center, of
an atom is made
up of two types
of particles:

Protons

Neutrons

Electrons revolve in
orbits around the nucleus.

Electric charge is one of the most important forces in nature. It is responsible for holding the atom together. There are two kinds of charges—positive and negative. The nucleus has a positive charge, and the electrons have a negative charge. Since opposite electric charges attract each other, the electrons are held in their orbits by the opposing force of the nucleus.

THE PARTS OF A NUCLEUS

Inside the nucleus are even smaller parts, or subatomic particles, called protons and neutrons. Protons carry the positive charge. Each element has a particular number of protons. If a nucleus contains only one proton, the element is hydrogen. If the nucleus contains 29 protons, the element is copper. Plutonium atoms have 94 protons.

An atom usually has the same number of protons in the nucleus as electrons moving around the nucleus. Since each proton carries a positive charge and each electron carries a negative charge, the charges are balanced.

Neutrons are about the same size as protons but do not have an electric charge. These particles are called neutrons because they are electrically neutral (neither positive nor negative).

Although the nucleus of a particular element must always have the same number of protons, it can have differing num-

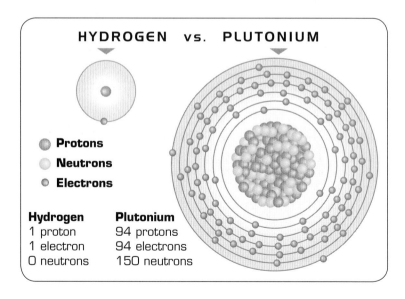

HYDROGEN vs. PLUTONIUM

- Protons
- Neutrons
- Electrons

Hydrogen	Plutonium
1 proton	94 protons
1 electron	94 electrons
0 neutrons	150 neutrons

bers of neutrons. Lighter elements, such as helium, usually have the same number of protons and neutrons. Heavier elements, such as uranium, have more neutrons than protons. Hydrogen usually has no neutrons at all.

Isotopes are forms of an element that have different numbers of neutrons in their nuclei. For example, there are three isotopes of hydrogen. The most abundant isotope, ordinary hydrogen, has one proton and no neutrons in its nucleus. Deuterium is the hydrogen isotope with one proton and one neutron, and tritium is the hydrogen isotope with one proton and two neutrons.

Nuclear reactors at a government site in Richland, Washington, are used to manufacture tritium for hydrogen bombs.

AMAZING ELECTRONS

Electrons do some of the most important "jobs" in nature. Electrons hold atoms together in molecules. Electrons also provide the electricity that turns on lights and operates computers. Electrons perform these jobs because of certain laws of nature that govern how they behave.

Electrons do not zip around the nucleus randomly. They stay in distinct orbits called shells. Imagine these shells as lanes in a running track. The electrons are like runners; they

Just as runners are assigned to a specific lane on a track, nature assigns electrons to a specific shell in an atom.

must stay in their assigned lane, or shell. The difference is that one shell can have several electrons.

In their orbital shells, electrons whirl around the nucleus of an atom billions of times per second. Imagine what a blur this would be if we could actually see an atom. Picture the whirling propeller on a small airplane. The propeller spins so fast that it creates the illusion of being a solid disk on the nose of the plane. The speeding electrons create a similar kind of blur around the atomic nucleus.

Although we cannot see electrons, we can see their effects all around us every day. The electrons in the outer shell of some atoms, such as copper, can be easily knocked out of orbit and away from the atom. These free electrons travel through

Copper wire is used in a variety of electronics and appliances.

> **DID YOU KNOW?**
>
> The word *atom* comes from *atomos*, a Greek word that means "uncuttable."

copper wire and create electric current, providing the power for the televisions, computers, lamps, and appliances we use daily.

Chemical reactions can cause some atoms to lose electrons. These atoms become positively charged because there are now more protons than electrons. Some atoms can gain more than their ordinary share of electrons. These atoms become negatively charged because there are now more electrons than protons. An atom with a positive or negative electric charge is called an ion.

WHERE DID ATOMS COME FROM?

Cosmologists, scientists who study the universe, theorize that all matter and energy exploded into being with an event they call the Big Bang. In that moment, the universe was too hot for ordinary matter to exist. There was nothing but energy. Immediately, the universe began to expand and cool, and matter began to take shape. First, simple bits of matter formed, which physicists call quarks. The quarks then joined to make protons and neutrons. Simple atoms of hydrogen and helium gas formed.

Next, clouds of gas came together to form galaxies and stars. Nuclear reactions inside the stars provided enough heat to make the stars shine. Many of the stars exploded, and the heat caused nuclei to fuse together, making the heavier elements. However, only about 1 percent of the atoms that exist today are heavier than hydrogen or helium.

Cosmologists believe that the universe was created by an astronomical event known as the Big Bang. The theory is based on the idea that the universe is still expanding from a central point.

Models of the Atom

The discovery of radioactivity gave scientists an important tool in creating an accurate model of an atom. Ernest Rutherford allowed a thin gold foil to be bombarded by particles. He found that most of the particles went through the foil, but a few bounced back. He concluded that the particles were bouncing off of a dense core, which he called the nucleus. Beyond the nucleus, he believed an atom was mostly empty space. Soon he and others discovered that the nucleus was made of even smaller protons and neutrons. In Rutherford's model of the atom, electrons orbited a small, dense nucleus. But in his model, the electrons would gradually lose altitude like a satellite orbiting Earth. What keeps the electrons from eventually crashing into the nucleus?

The answer came from studies of light and the new science of quantum mechanics. Danish physicist Niels Bohr came up with the idea that each electron was "assigned" an orbit at a particular distance from the nucleus. He called these distances "energy levels." An electron could go from one energy level to another, but it had to jump, not glide or slide. An electron could jump to a higher energy level by absorbing a packet of electromagnetic energy called a quantum. When it fell back to its assigned level, it gave off a quantum of light.

In Bohr's model, the electrons orbited the nucleus in

orbital shells. However, scientists working in quantum mechanics later made this model more accurate. They found electrons could behave like a wave. In orbit, the electron created a wave like a plucked guitar string.

Physicists found that they could not predict exactly where an electron might be at a given time. They could only figure the probability of the electron's location. In the new model of the atom, the electron occupies a cloudlike space around the nucleus.

Each electron in Bohr's model of the atom followed a separate, definite path.

The Chemical World of Molecules

ATOMS OF DIFFERENT elements can join to make molecules. A molecule made up of different kinds of atoms is called a chemical compound.

A molecule is the smallest possible amount of a compound. Large molecules may be broken down into simpler, smaller molecules, and

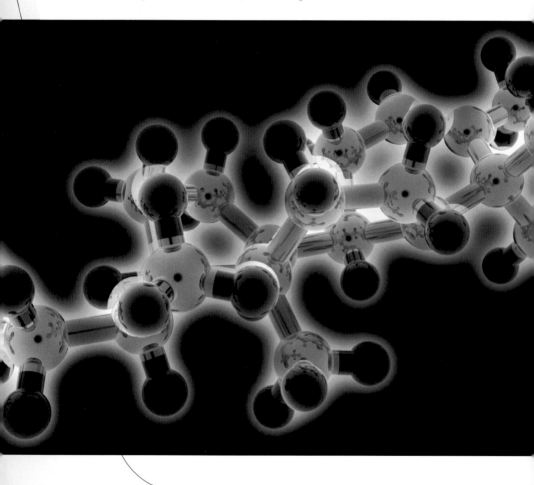

Molecules are created from multiple atoms in a certain arrangement.

the smallest molecules may be broken down into the atoms that form them. For example, water molecules may be converted to hydrogen and oxygen, the two elements that make up water.

All chemistry is based on molecules coming together and splitting apart. Only certain types of elements can join to create a compound. Two metals cannot join to make a compound, but metals can join with certain nonmetals to create compounds. For example, atoms of iron can join with atoms of oxygen to make a compound called iron oxide, which is rust.

One molecule of iron oxide, or rust, is made up of one atom of iron and one atom of oxygen.

Atoms can join to create molecules because their electrons create bonds. Only atoms that can accept or donate electrons form bonds. There are two basic kind of bonds—ionic and covalent.

Some bonds are made when a positive ion joins with a negative ion. The positive and negative charges attract and hold the ions together to form an ionic bond. Sodium chloride, or table salt, is made of positive sodium ions and negative chlorine ions that are attracted to each other.

Some bonds are made when two atoms share two elec-

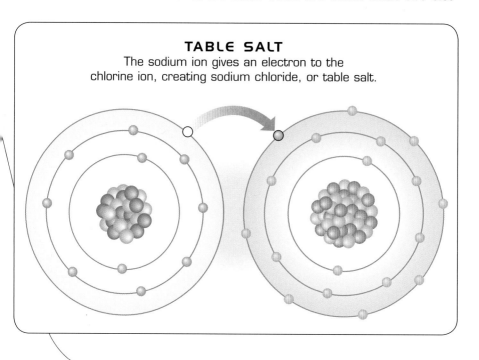

TABLE SALT
The sodium ion gives an electron to the chlorine ion, creating sodium chloride, or table salt.

trons, one from each atom. The two electrons orbit both nuclei. This is called a covalent bond. The simplest example of a covalent bond is the hydrogen molecule, which is made of two hydrogen atoms. Each hydrogen atom contributes its single electron to form an electron pair, which orbit both hydrogen atoms. Sugar is a compound that is made up of covalent bonds between atoms of carbon, hydrogen, and oxygen.

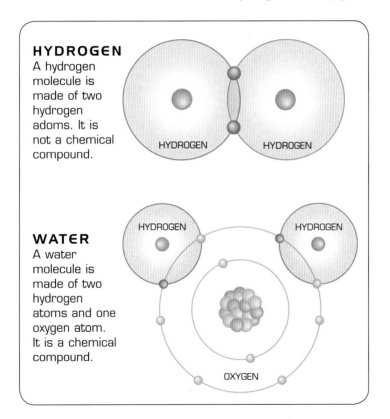

HYDROGEN
A hydrogen molecule is made of two hydrogen adoms. It is not a chemical compound.

HYDROGEN   HYDROGEN

WATER
A water molecule is made of two hydrogen atoms and one oxygen atom. It is a chemical compound.

HYDROGEN   HYDROGEN

OXYGEN

Organizing Atoms

In the early 1800s, an English chemist named John Dalton used mathematics to determine a property that he called atomic weight. The atomic weight of each atom was different. Atomic weight explained why atoms always combined in the same proportions to create various substances.

In the late 1800s, a Russian scientist named Dimitri Ivanovich Mendeleev grouped elements by their atomic weights to create the periodic table of the elements. After placing the elements in the table, he found that elements with similar properties occur in regular patterns in the table. At the time, scientists had discovered 63 elements. There were gaps in the table, and Mendeleev predicted that other elements would be discovered to fill the gaps. He was right. By the end of the 1900s, scientists had discovered more than 110 elements, most of which occur in nature. They had also created some artificial elements, such as neptunium and einsteinium.

In his periodic table, Dimitri Mendeleev arranged elements with similar properties into groups.

INORGANIC AND ORGANIC MOLECULES

Molecules can be divided into two main types, inorganic and organic. Inorganic molecules are found mainly in nonliving things. Rocks, for example, are made of inorganic molecules.

Organic molecules contain carbon and are found in things that are living or were once alive. Animal and plant tissues contain organic compounds. Coal, petroleum, natural gas, and other fossil fuels also contain organic molecules. These fossil fuels formed from plants and animals that were alive millions of years ago. The molecules found in fossil fuels are called hydrocarbons because they contain the chemical elements hydrogen and carbon.

Coal, as well as other fossil fuels, is used to provide the fuel needed to run many types of power plants.

WHAT MOLECULES DO

Molecules are capable of doing many things. Some molecules make up useful objects, such as plastic computer cases, woolen sweaters, and metal car parts. Other molecules do important jobs. A red molecule called hemoglobin carries oxygen in the blood from the lungs to every tissue in the human body. Other molecules act as chemical messengers, carrying signals from one nerve cell to another.

One of the most important molecules is a long, thin molecule called deoxyribonucleic acid (DNA). The genes—basic units of heredity—of every living thing are made of DNA. This master molecule of life determines what all organisms look like and how they function.

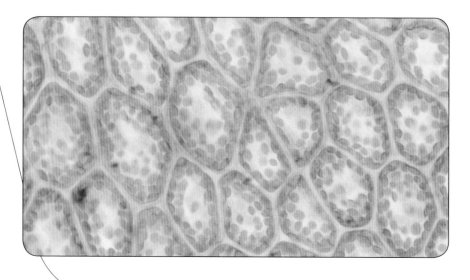

Green molecules in plants called chlorophyll make food by absorbing energy from sunlight in a process called photosynthesis.

How Atoms and Molecules Change

ATOMS AND MOLECULES can go through many changes, but they always follow one important law of nature. The law of the conservation of matter and energy, discovered in the 1700s by French chemist Antoine Lavoisier, states that matter and energy cannot be created or destroyed; they can only be changed.

A substance can change from a solid to a liquid to a gas and still be the same substance. This kind of change is called physical change. Molecules in a substance can also break apart and come together in a different way to form new substances. This kind of change is called chemical change. The nucleus of some elements can change into the nucleus of another element, changing a small amount of matter into energy. This kind of nuclear change is called transmutation.

Because of his contributions to the field of chemistry, Lavoisier is known by most scientists as the father of modern chemistry.

DID YOU KNOW?

Ernest Rutherford, a scientist who was awarded the Nobel Prize in chemistry in 1908, achieved the first artificial transmutation by changing nitrogen into oxygen.

PHYSICAL CHANGE

Like a fidgety child, atoms and molecules cannot keep still. They are in constant motion, absorbing and giving off heat energy. The more heat energy an atom or molecule absorbs, the faster it moves.

The speed with which molecules move around determines whether the substance is a solid, liquid, or gas. Scientists call solids, liquids, and gases states of matter. A substance does not change into a new substance when it changes its state of matter. The same molecules that make up liquid water, for example, make up solid ice cubes from a freezer, as well as the gas (steam) that rises from a pot of boiling water.

Molecules are always in motion, but adding heat energy makes molecules move around even faster. The more the molecules move around, the farther they move from one another. In ice, water molecules move around less and are close enough to make a solid. Adding heat causes the molecules to move farther from one another, and the solid ice turns into liquid

STATES OF MATTER

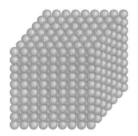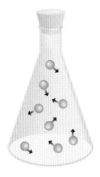

SOLID

Solid objects, such as a block of wood, are made of molecules that are packed closely together. These molecules vibrate. Solids have their own definite shapes.

LIQUID

Liquids like water are made of molecules that are farther apart and move around each other. Liquids take the shapes of their containers.

GAS

Gas molecules, like oxygen, move freely in all directions, usually at high speeds. They expand to completely fill whatever container they are in.

water. Adding more heat, as happens when a pot of water is set on a hot stove, makes the molecules fly in all directions. The liquid then turns to water vapor.

CHEMICAL CHANGE

The making and breaking of chemical bonds cause new molecules to form. These new molecules are completely new substances. This process is called a chemical reaction. Compounds of sulfur and oxygen or nitrogen and oxygen are given off in smoke from factories that burn fossil fuels. These compounds react with water in the air to form acids, which results in acid rain.

The creation of new substances, however, strictly follows the law of the conservation of matter. Scientists proved this by weighing substances before and after a chemical reaction.

Acid rain can have a devastating effect on the environment. The needles of a pine tree damaged by acid rain (left) look pale and withered in comparison to those on a healthy branch.

Lavoisier was the first scientist to weigh all of the reactants before and products after a reaction. He determined that the total weights of the reactants and the products were the same.

For example, if you mix vinegar and baking soda, you will get a bubbling chemical reaction. The bubbles come from carbon dioxide gas that forms from the chemical reaction. Suppose you weigh the vinegar and baking soda, conduct the experiment, and trap the carbon dioxide bubbles in a container. When you weigh the gas and the leftover liquid, you would find that they weigh the same as the vinegar and baking soda with which you started the experiment. The chemicals change into new substances, but the total amount of matter stays the same.

Lavoisier was able to prove his theory of the conservation of matter through experiments with chemical reactions.

Polymers and Plastics

One type of molecule that brought about major changes in modern life is the polymer. Polymers are made of molecules that repeat over and over again. A polymer is like a train made up of dozens of identical railroad cars hooked together.

The plastics used to make picnic cups and plates, computer cases, outdoor furniture, toys, soda bottles, garbage bags, and thousands of other things you use every day are made from polymers. The chemical process of hooking the molecules together is called polymerization.

Since the mid-1800s, chemists have been working on making synthetic (artificial) molecules. They have experimented with cellulose, a natural chemical in plants. Using cellulose, chemists invented rayon and cellophane wrap.

In 1907, a Belgian chemist in New York City invented the first true artificial plastic. His name was Leo Hendrik Baekeland, and he called his chemical "Bakelite." This sticky substance could be molded and hardened into various shapes. One of the first uses for Bakelite was in billiard balls. It was then used for handles on knives, forks, and spoons. It was also a good insulator for electrical connectors. The invention of nylon and many other kinds of plastics followed.

One of the most useful plastics, polyethylene, was discovered in 1933. It was accidentally made by researchers experi-

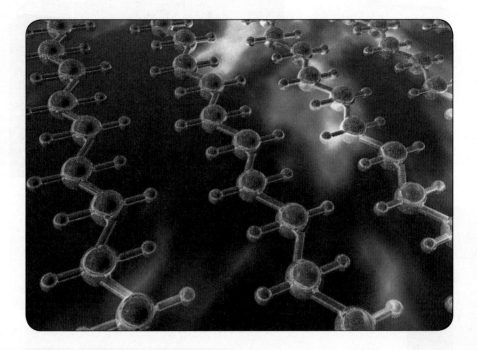

menting with petroleum products. Polyethylene has many uses because it is strong and lightweight.

Today, plastic polymers are made from petroleum in oil refineries. The petroleum is heated in furnaces where chemicals are added to give the long chains of molecules certain properties, such as strength and flexibility. The polymers are heated and then cooled and chopped into small pieces called pellets. The pellets are shipped to manufacturers, where they are melted and molded into various plastic products.

Long chains of hydrocarbons are used to create plastics, such as polyethylene.

NUCLEAR CHANGE

Changes can also occur in the nucleus of an atom. Sometimes the nucleus of one kind of element gives off subatomic particles, such as alpha or beta particles, and transforms into the nucleus of another element. An alpha particle is the same as a helium nucleus—it is made of two protons and two neutrons. A beta particle is an electron. Atoms give off these particles, which is called nuclear radiation. When a nucleus gives off nuclear radiation, the change is called radioactive decay.

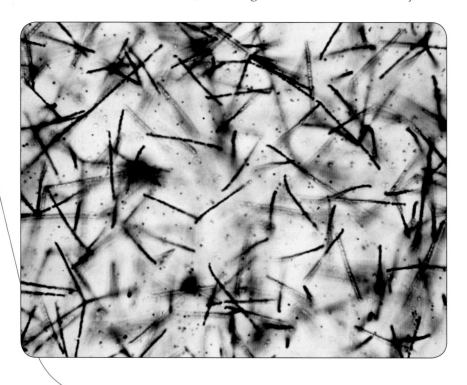

Alpha particles are tracked during radioactive decay.

Only certain kinds of atoms can decay naturally. Naturally radioactive atoms are isotopes of heavy atoms, such as uranium, radium, and plutonium. When these atoms decay, they release alpha and beta particles and rays of energy called gamma rays. Gamma rays are a form of radiation called electromagnetic radiation. Light is also a form of electromagnetic radiation. Gamma rays, however, have much more energy than visible light rays.

Radioactive decay is measured in half-life—the amount of time it takes for half of the amount of an element to decay. Some elements have a half-life of only a few seconds. Other

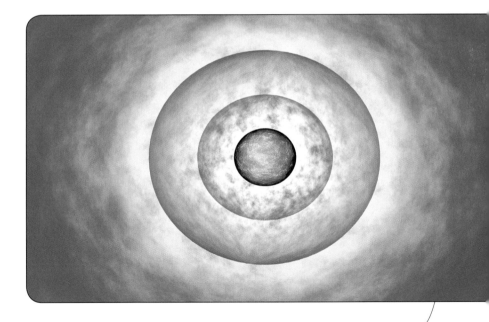

Special detectors have recorded gamma ray bursts coming from objects in deep space.

elements decay much more slowly. An isotope of uranium called U-235 (named after the number of protons and neutrons in its nucleus) has a half-life of about 700 million years. After 700 million years, half of the U-235 would have changed into a different isotope. Eventually, U-235 changes into lead.

In nuclear reactions, the law of conservation of matter does not apply. Some of the matter is converted into energy. The large amount of energy released by some nuclear reactions is used in power plants. The reaction itself does not generate electricity, but the energy from the reaction creates heat, boiling the water that drives turbines within the power plants. These turbines generate the electricity.

A sample of U-235 weighing 10 pounds (4.5 kilograms) is used to manufacture nuclear weapon components.

Studying Atoms and Molecules

IF ATOMS AND MOLECULES are too small to see, how did scientists learn so much about them? Physicists and chemists use some unique ways to find out about atoms and molecules. Chemists learn about atoms, elements, and compounds by doing experiments and building models of molecules on computers. They also used the periodic table to predict new elements.

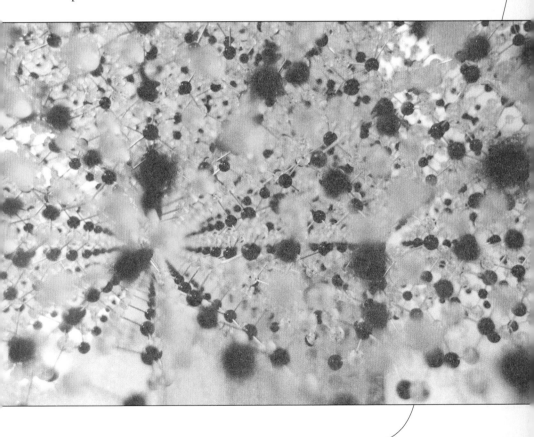

A molecule model features the structure of quartz (silicon dioxide). The crystalline form repeats the same basic quartz molecule (3 silicon atoms and 6 oxygen atoms) over and over.

From their study of molecules, chemists learned to make new compounds. New medicines, plastics, fertilizers, computer chips, textiles, and other useful materials have been made by chemists who understand the structure of molecules.

A cyclotron, a machine capable of producing isotopes, is crucial for scientific research.

X-RAYING MOLECULES

Light rays strike and bounce off objects, allowing us to see the objects with our eyes. Scientists use tools with other, more powerful kinds of rays, such as X-rays, to see inside atoms and molecules. They use a technique called X-ray crystallography to find out where atoms are in a crystal. A crystal is a solid molecule, and all the atoms in a crystal line up in a regular pattern, like a marching band on a field. When an X-ray strikes an atom in a crystal, the ray bounces off and makes a pattern on photographic film.

Scientists have made very important discoveries using X-ray crystallography. For example, they discovered that the DNA molecule has the shape of a twisted ladder.

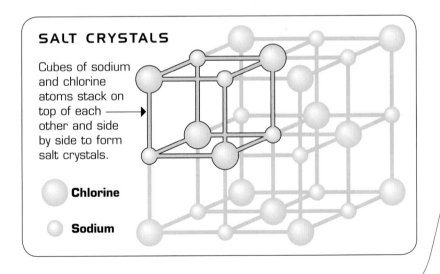

SALT CRYSTALS

Cubes of sodium and chlorine atoms stack on top of each other and side by side to form salt crystals. ⟶

Chlorine

Sodium

The Curies: An Atomic Family

Marie Sklodowska Curie (1867–1934) was a Polish woman who moved to Paris, became a physicist, and married another French physicist named Pierre Curie. The Curies did research on radioactivity in the 1890s.

Radioactivity had been accidentally discovered by French physicist Henri Becquerel in 1896. He found that some uranium ore left in a dark desk drawer made an image on photographic plates. He concluded that the uranium gave off

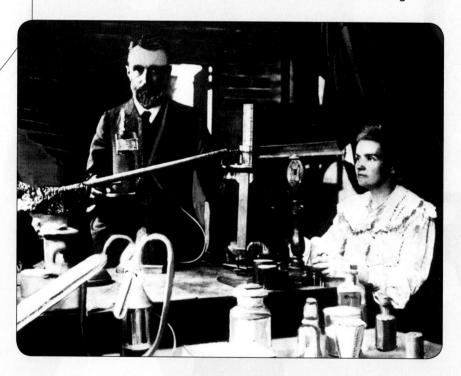

Pierre and Marie Curie performed experiments in radioactivity in a laboratory.

mysterious radiation, not unlike the X-rays discovered the year before by German physicist Wilhelm Conrad Roentgen.

The Curies studied this mysterious radiation. Marie correctly believed that radiation came from individual atoms. The Curies dug through tons of uranium ore and found two more radioactive elements, radium and polonium. In 1903, the Curies and Becquerel won the Nobel Prize for their work on radiation. Pierre Curie died, but Marie went on to win a second Nobel Prize in chemistry in 1911 for the discovery of radium and polonium.

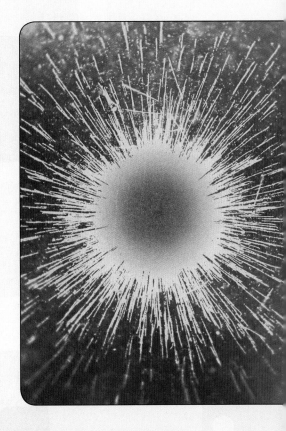

The Curies' daughter, Irene Joliot-Curie, also became a famous atomic physicist. She and her husband, Frederic, won the 1935 Nobel Prize for creating artificial radioactive elements. The Joliot-Curies helped design the first French atomic reactors for producing nuclear energy.

Alpha particles are emitted from a sample of radium, a powerful radioactive substance.

SMASHING ATOMS

Physicists use huge machines called particle accelerators to find out what atoms are made of. Some accelerators are long tubes, while others are round rings.

Physicists use beams of electrons or protons traveling at high speed inside these particle accelerators to "see" inside atoms. The beam smashes into protons and neutrons and breaks them into tinier pieces. Because the particles are so small, the physicists must use magnets, computers, and other devices to record what happens. The recording devices are called particle detectors.

The first detectors were cloud chambers and bubble chambers. A cloud chamber was filled with gas, and a bubble chamber contained an extremely hot liquid. When a subatomic particle passed through a cloud chamber, it created a visible trail of liquid droplets. A subatomic particle passing through the extremely hot liquid created tiny bubbles. Physicists took

DID YOU KNOW?

The European Center for Nuclear Research is the world's largest particle physics laboratory. Located in Geneva, Switzerland, the center is operated by 6,500 scientists from around the world.

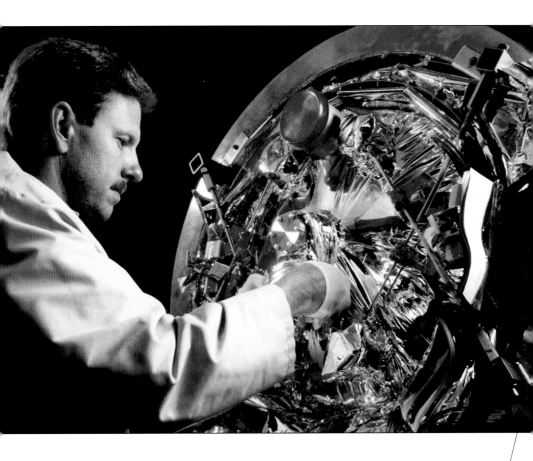

pictures of the particle trails so they could study them.

Today's particle accelerators use detectors that record either electrical charges or faint flashes of light caused by the particles striking the detector. Using such devices, physicists have learned that protons and neutrons are made of three quarks apiece. The quarks are held together by a power-

A scientist used a particle accelerator to closely study the subatomic particles known as quarks.

ful nuclear force called the strong force. The strong force is behind the enormous power of an atomic explosion.

Physicists have also discovered many subatomic particles that may have existed at the birth of the universe. Now they wonder if quarks are made of even smaller particles. With newer and more powerful atom smashers, perhaps they will find out.

The paths of subatomic particles were tracked using a particle accelerator at a laboratory in Geneva, Switzerland. Any charged particle passing through the liquid left behind a trail of tiny bubbles.

alpha particle—a helium atom nucleus that is ejected from the nucleus of a radioactive atom

beta particle—an electron that is ejected from the nucleus of a radioactive atom

bonds—the exchange or sharing of electrons by atoms to form a molecule

charge—a property of subatomic particles, such as protons and electrons, that can be positive or negative

electrons—negatively charged particles that orbit an atomic nucleus

element—a substance made of atoms with the same number of protons in their nuclei

inorganic molecule—a molecule that does not contain the element carbon

ion—an electrically charged atom

isotopes—atoms that have the same number of protons but different numbers of neutrons in the nucleus

mass—the amount of matter that a substance contains

matter—the stuff of which all things in the universe are made

neutrons—tiny particles inside an atom's nucleus; a neutron is about the same size as a proton and has no electric charge

nucleus—the dense core of an atom

organic molecule—a molecule that contains the element carbon, which is found in all living things

particle accelerators—machines that speed up subatomic particles to near the speed of light and use them to smash into and break apart atoms for study

protons—tiny particles inside an atom's nucleus; a proton has a positive electric charge

quarks—tiny particles that make up protons and neutrons

radioactive decay—the giving off of subatomic particles by an atom

transmutation—the changing of one element into another

▸ Physicists group elements according to certain numbers. The atomic number is the number of protons in the element's atomic nucleus. The atomic mass number is the total of the protons and the neutrons in a nucleus.

▸ There are 111 internationally recognized elements. Physicists claim to have found an additional five elements. All of the elements with atomic numbers above 92 (the number of uranium) are called transuranium elements. Transuranium elements do not exist in nature. They were made by physicists in particle accelerators.

▸ Electrons orbit the nucleus of an atom in distinct shells. There can be up to seven shells. Physicists have numbered the shells 1 through 7. The shells are also called K, L, M, N, O, P, and Q. The outer shell, number 7, can hold up to 98 electrons. However, the outer shells are rarely filled.

▸ Just as removing heat from atoms causes them to slow down, slowing down the motion of atoms makes them colder. If a scientist could stop an atom from moving even a slight bit, the temperature of the atom would be absolute zero (-459.67 degrees Fahrenheit or -273.15 degrees Celsius). This hypothetical temperature, which has never been reached, is the coldest anything could possibly be.

▸ A few elements resist bonding with other elements. These elements are the gases argon, helium, krypton, neon, radon, and xenon. These six elements are called noble gases.

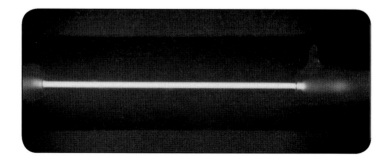

A glass tube containing neon gas emitted a red-orange glow after voltage was applied. Different colors occur when other noble gases are added to the tube.

At the Library

Gore, Bryson. *Physics: A Hair Is Wider Than a Million Atoms.*
 Mankato, Minn.: Stargazer Books, 2006.
Juettner, Bonnie. *Molecules.* Farmington Hills, Mich.: Kidhaven
 Press, 2005.
Solway, Andrew. *A History of Super Science.* Chicago: Raintree, 2006.
Stewart, Melissa. *Atoms.* Minneapolis: Compass Point Books, 2003.
Woodford, Chris, and Martin Clowes. *Atoms and Molecules.* San
 Diego: Blackbirch Press, 2004.

On the Web

For more information on this topic, use FactHound.
 1. Go to *www.facthound.com*
 2. Type in this book ID: 0756519608
 3. Click on the *Fetch It* button.
FactHound will find the best Web sites for you.

On the Road

National Museum of Nuclear
Science and History
 1905 Mountain Road N.W.
 Albuquerque, NM 87104
 505/245-2137

Matter and Molecules Exhibit
Science Museum of Virginia
 2500 W. Broad St.
 Richmond, VA 23220
 800/659-1727

Explore all the Physical Science books

Atoms & Molecules: Building
Blocks of the Universe

Chemical Change: From Fireworks
to Rust

Manipulating Light: Reflection,
Refraction, and Absorption

The Periodic Table: Mapping the
Elements

Physical Change: Reshaping
Matter

Waves: Energy on the Move

A complete list of Exploring Science titles is available
on our Web site: *www.compasspointbooks.com*